The Boundary

A Play

Tom Stoppard
and
Clive Exton

Samuel French – London
New York – Toronto – Hollywood

ISBN 0 573 12046 3

Please see page iv for further copyright information.

THE BOUNDARY

First produced by the BBC on July 19th 1975, for Eleventh Hour with the following cast of characters:

Johnson	Michael Aldridge
Bunyans	Frank Thornton
Brenda	Elvi Hale
Voice of the telephone operator	Jean Channon
Brenda's double	Olive McNeil
1st cricketer	Barry Summerford
2nd cricketer	Gordon Hann
The voices of	John Arlott and Trevor Bailey

Directed by Mike Newell
Produced by Graeme McDonald

The action takes place in a lexicographer's library

Time—the present

CHARACTERS

Johnson
Bunyans
Brenda
1st Cricketer
2nd Cricketer

Other plays by Tom Stoppard
published by Samuel French Ltd:

Albert's Bridge
Artist Descending a Staircase
Dirty Linen and New-Found-Land
The Fifteen Minute Hamlet
Hapgood
If You're Glad I'll Be Frank
Night and Day
The Real Inspector Hound
The Real Thing
Rosencrantz and Guildenstern Are Dead
A Separate Peace

THE BOUNDARY

A lexicographer's library

The room contains a desk, a table and a chair. Around the walls are bookshelves filled with boxes. There is also a copy of "Fowler's Modern English Usage". The room is cluttered with the paraphernalia of the life work of our heroes. Paper is everywhere but the disorder seems exaggerated; in fact, chaos reigns. It seems that the place has been turned over. There are piles of paper on the floor and over the furniture, beneath which are hidden a television set, a telescope on a tripod, a telephone, a typewriter and a woman. Against the door is a drift of paper, like a snowdrift. Through the french windows we see a cricketer, who figures intermittently throughout the play as a white flannelled sentinel. A pane of glass in the french windows is broken. From nowhere in particular comes the modulated, well-bred sound of a TV cricket post-mortem

The door is pushed open inwards and Johnson, who is an old man, enters, knee-deep in slips of papers. He registers the unwelcome fact that his room has been pillaged and becomes more and more concerned and horrified. He picks slips of paper up here and there and mutters to himself ...

Johnson Tannin ... Therefore ... Talismanical ... Tortoise ... Telephone ...

He searches in a mound of paper and scoops up an armful, revealing a small television set, with a cricket match going on. At the same time he announces triumphantly ...

Telephone ...

We become aware of the source of the sound. He taps on top of the TV set with his hand

Operator ...! Operator ...!

Realizing his mistake, he drops the papers back on the TV set. He then begins searching for the phone under another pile of papers. He lifts up another armful, revealing a telescope on a tripod. He pauses and studies it for a moment. He's puzzled, he has lost track of his thought. He puts his eye to the telescope, which is pointing through the window in a slightly downward direction. Immediately afterwards he realizes that he still has the wrong implement and drops the papers over the telescope. His mind clears. An old-fashioned telephone is sitting in the middle of a table. He puts the receiver to his ear, thinks for a moment, dials three digits . . .

Operator (*off; speaking through a crackle*) Telegrams.
Johnson I wanted directory enquiries.
Operator (*off; speaking through a crackle*) A telegram to directory enquiries?
Johnson No, I'd rather speak to them if that's possible.
Operator (*off; speaking through a crackle*) Directory enquiries is one-nine-two.
Johnson Thank you. (*He hangs up and dials again*)
Operator (*through crackling*) Directory. Which town?
Johnson Can you get me the telephone number of the police.
Operator (*through crackling*) Is it an emergency?
Johnson Emergency. Well, yes.
Operator (*through crackling*) Dial nine nine nine.
Johnson Thank you. (*He replaces the receiver and dials 999*)
Operator (*through crackling*) Emergency. Which service?
Johnson Now look here, my name is Johnson. I seem to have been bungled. (*Pause*) Just a moment. (*He hangs up absent-mindedly, crosses to a pile of galleyproofs and rummages among it. He comes up with the one he wants, remarking victoriously*) Burgled.

He turns back to the phone but before he reaches it:

The door opens and Bunyans enters

Burglars.
Bunyans I beg your pardon.
Johnson Look.
Bunyans (*softly to himself*) Bugger.
Johnson Burglars.

Bunyans Anything missing?

They look around at the chaos

Johnson Not at first glance, but even so . . . the year's work . . . (*In despair he picks up a galleyproof*)
Bunyans Any sign of entry?
Johnson (*glancing at the galleyproof*) Yes, that's here. (*Reading*) Entry . . . Entune . . . Enturret . . . Entwine . . .
Bunyans No, I mean . . .
Johnson Ah . . . The door wasn't locked.
Bunyans It's not necessarily a burglary.
Johnson No. No. Possibly housebreaking if the act was committed during the hours of daylight.

Bunyans turns aside, picks up a handful of papers and reads them

Bunyans Triangle . . . Tuffett . . . Tendon . . .
Johnson What are you doing?
Bunyans Refiling.
Johnson As if nothing had happened?
Bunyans How else would we know if anything is missing? (*He picks up a slip*) Tactile . . . Taclobo to Tailor . . . Taclobo to Tailor . . .

Bunyans wanders around the room repeating "Taclobo to Tailor" until he finds the box. He holds it aloft triumphantly, puts it on the long table in the centre of the room and carefully puts the slip of paper into it

Johnson meanwhile has picked up another slip of paper from the floor

Johnson Tardel.
Bunyans No. No. We're looking for Taclobo to Tailor.
Johnson Ah. (*He allows the slip of paper to flutter to the ground*)

Bunyans is picking up slips and letting them drop again

Bunyans Telpher. . . . Tie-wigged. . . . Take-off. . . . Tentative. . . .

Tush.... Tea-time.... Thyration.... Toadstool.... Titanic.... (*He picks up the end of a piece of paper which is uniquely long and reads*) The ...

Johnson is staring, puzzled, at the mess

Johnson Terrible.
Bunyans Tercel-gentel to Tazkere.
Johnson No I mean, it's just terrible, who can have done this?

They both stop what they're doing and shake their heads, puzzled

Bunyans It's a mystery.
Johnson A religious truth known only from divine revelation?
Bunyans I think not. More prosaic. A matter unexplained or inexplicable. A riddle or enigma. (*He picks up another slip*) ... Telinga. (*He drops it*)
Johnson This is the wrong method. We must collect the boxes and then pick up at random.
Bunyans Ah. Of course! The boxes first.

He starts to collect boxes. Johnson helps him

Johnson Put them in order on the table. T to Tacky; Taclobo to Tailor; Tailorage to Talent ...
Bunyans Tales to Tampon.

They start to assemble the boxes in the long row on the table

Bunyans Where's Brenda?
Johnson Breezey to Bretheren.
Bunyans No. No. Your wife.

Johnson stops working and looks suspicously at Bunyans, who carries on working

Johnson Why?

Bunyans stops and looks at Johnson guiltily

Bunyans Nothing. No reason. I wondered. One wonders. (*He picks up another box insouciantly*) Tell to Temptress.
Johnson (*angrily*) What do you imply?
Bunyans (*showing the box*) The box.
Johnson (*sarcastically*) Conveniently to hand.
Bunyans (*wearily*) Oh—Johnson ... The boxes. The boxes.

They both go back to their work

Johnson We had a spat at lunch.
Bunyans Spawn of oyster? And a glass of Hock?
Johnson Not at all. We'd already had a spat over breakfast.
Bunyans A pair of spats ... Abbreviation of spatterdash, seventeenth century ... short gaiter covering instep at lunch, and another at breakfast.
Johnson Tiff.
Bunyans What was it about?
Johnson "O".
Bunyans Oh what?
Johnson Her "O". You saw her "O"?
Bunyans Oh, "O"—her "O". No.
Johnson She got osculate down as a moving staircase.
Bunyans Did you tell her?
Johnson I showed her.
Bunyans What did she say?
Johnson She said Chambers was a fool, and Webster taken in by Chambers.
Bunyans (*picking up a slip*) Trollop.
Johnson (*bridling*) What?
Bunyans (*with another slip*) Tart ...
Johnson By God no, now look here ...
Bunyans (*calmly with third slip*) Trans-substantiation.

They continue to work

You had a spat or tiff. She went off in a huff. Next thing we know, chaos and no Brenda.
Johnson Are you implying?
Bunyans You know Brenda as well as I do.
Johnson (*bridling*) Rather better I trust.

Bunyans Oh, much better. Much, much, much better. (*Intimately*) That's my point—inside-leg job. This was obviously an inside job.

Johnson You really think Brenda could have done this? Out of spite?

Bunyans "Hell hath no fury like a" ... (*He pauses, forgetting the quotation*)

Johnson Woman.

Bunyans No—begins with "S".

Johnson Scorned.

Bunyans Scorned.

Johnson Scorned? (*Accusingly*) Have you been scorning Brenda?

Bunyans Never. Constantly.

Johnson When did you scorn her?

Bunyans I am scorning her all the time, that's why she's done this. All that American rubbish she wanted in. Remember last year, splash-down. It was I who scorned her splash-down, and I was very scornful with it ... and go.

Johnson Go?

Bunyans (*witheringly*) Nineteen sixty-nine. When she put in go as a noun. We have go.

Johnson (*suddenly*) You said "inside breast".

Bunyans No, I didn't. I said leg—I mean job—inside job.

Johnson (*accusingly*) Tassanova.

Bunyans (*puzzled*) Tassanova?

Johnson V.E. night ...

Bunyans Tulipomania.

Johnson What?

Bunyans Obsession with tulips. Mainly Dutch.

Johnson You surprise me.

Bunyans Astonish. Amaze.

Johnson Pedant. (*He picks up another slip*) Train.

Bunyans Trachelipod to Traitor. Box twenty-eight.

Johnson puts the slip into the box. He stands for a moment looking down at it in a reverie

Johnson Brenda used to love trains.

Bunyans Used to?

Johnson During the war. The blacked-out windows. The dim blue lights. Rocking through the night. (*Tartly*) But you know all about that, of course.

Bunyans Not at all.

Johnson Gammon! Bosh! Tingle-tangle.

Bunyans I know nothing of trains.

Johnson Oh no! Oh no! Does Brize Norton mean nothing to you? The *Goat and Whistle*?

Bunyans Nothing.

Johnson And what about V.E. night?

Bunyans Nothing.

Johnson I searched for you. I searched high and low for you.

Bunyans Nothing!

Johnson I stopped sailors in the street to inquire your whereabouts.

Bunyans We were in the amusement arcade. After we lost you in the hokey-cokey, we went to the amusement arcade.

Johnson Well-named indeed. And then?

Bunyans We waited an hour and a half and then I took her home.

Johnson Twaddle!

Bunyans She was at home when you got there, wasn't she?

Johnson At three in the morning certainly, feigning sleep. I have turned a blind eye, Bu'Nyans, to your lasciviousness for the sake of the dictionary. I had hoped that you too might share my joy in its creation, and that we might carry our bats together to the end of the innings. But you've gone too far now with your greasy denials of your knowledge of trains and Brize Norton.

Bunyans It happened thirty years ago, Johnson.

Johnson What happened?

Bunyans (*helplessly*) Nothing happened. Oh Johnson . . .

Johnson Don't Johnson me, Bunyans. (*He pronounces it like the edible rounded bulb of allium cepa*)

Bunyans (*bridling*) Have a care, Johnson.

Johnson Bunyans. Bunyans. Bunyans.

Bunyans Bu'Nyans.

Johnson Bunyans. And there's an end to it. Transparent.

Bunyans Box thirty.

Johnson turns, crosses upstage a little, stoops to pick up a slip and turns downstage

Johnson Trampoline. An elastic contrivance resembling a spring mattress. Oh God! Oh, God! (*He hurls the slip from him and collapses into a sitting position on the floor, rocking back and forth and weeping noisily*) Oh God! Oh God!
Bunyans (*looking discomforted*) Oh, Fowler ... come on, F. Oh, Johnson ... come on, Johnson ... It was nothing.
Johnson Oh, God in heaven, help me!

Bunyans crosses to him awkwardly, leans down and pats his head

Bunyans Nothing.
Johnson Look around you, Bu'Nyans, a year's work. We can never re-assemble it in time!

Bunyans crouches beside Johnson and puts a hand on his shoulder

Bunyans What's a year?
Johnson I'm not young. Who did this to us, Bu'Nyans?
Bunyans (*shaking his head*) Come on, Johnson—take heart. You know you can lean on me.
Johnson Very well—yes, my dear chap—(*he leans on Bunyans*) your support has always been—

Down they go in a heap

Now then.
Bunyans I'm sorry. (*He gets stiffly to his feet*) I'm sorry. (*He extends a hand down to help Johnson*)
Johnson I'll just stay here for a bit. Until I feel up to the mark.
Bunyans Good. Take a rest. You've been over-doing it.

He goes back towards the central table and starts picking up slips again

Johnson lies quite still for a moment and then picks up a slip that lies on a pile about eighteen inches from his nose

Johnson (*reading*) Tit.

He groans and throws it aside. In moving this slip he has revealed something which puzzles him. He squinnies at it. He can't make it out. Without otherwise moving he moves another slip. A woman's foot is revealed wearing an open-toed sandal—the foot having bunions. The toe is pointing at the ceiling. He looks nervously across at Bunyans who has his back to him

(*To himself*) Bunions . . .
Bunyans Bu'Nyans . . .

Johnson covers the foot

Bunyans casually picks up a galley off the floor

Here are some more of her "O"s.
Johnson (*cautiously*) Did Brenda have bunions?
Bunyans Yes.
Johnson How would you know!
Bunyans It's the talk of Bognor during the shrimping season. Good God—I see what you're getting at. (*Reading off a galleyproof*) Octaroon—small biscuit of ground almonds, white of egg, sugar . . . (*He throws away the galleyproof violently*) I could kill her.
Johnson I've just had a terrible thought. Where's the "M"s?

They both search the galleys

I thought as much—macaroon: noun—a wheaten paste made into long thin tubes and dried—Italian. Eighteenth century dandy. (*He looks further up the proof and reads off*) Macaroni—small American film star, male, twentieth century.

They stare at each other aghast

Bunyans (*faintly*) You don't think . . .?
Johnson We'd better look.

Bunyans searches for the "R" for Rooney proof while Johnson, more alert to Brenda's foibles, takes down the "M" proof

Bunyans No, it's all right, it goes straight from Roomy to Roop.

Johnson meanwhile has found it

Johnson No, it's here—run together as one word. (*He reads*) Mickeyrooney: a small egg-shaped wind instrument with a terracotta body; a whistle-like mouthpiece and finger holes. (*Pause*) Ocarina!

Bunyans (*reading off the galley*) Person of one-eighth negro blood. This is where we came in—octaroon.

Johnson It could be an honest mistake. This is where we came in, octaroon.

Bunyans (*furious*) This is deliberate sabotage. We've probably only scratched the surface of her lexicographic caprice—it is you and I on our own from now on.

Johnson That is all too evident, Bu'Nyans, but somewhat extreme as a solution.

Bunyans Your trouble, Johnson, has always been sentimentality.

Johmson No doubt, but common, human decency——

Bunyans (*picking up a slip*) Trogladite, thigh. (*He puts it in a box*)

Johnson (*picking up a slip*) Tremor. (*He pauses*) The fact of the matter is, Bu'Nyans, we're better off without her. I'll tell you something I've never told anyone before, Bu'Nyans.

Bunyans Yes.

Johnson is side-tracked by the cricket match

Johnson There's a window broken. It's those damned bounders.

Bunyans (*correcting*) Boundaries.

Johnson (*bitterly*) Hooked over square leg.

Bunyans Bouncers.

Johnson Damn cricket.

The cricket diversion ends

She never liked ... you know what.

Bunyans She loved it.

Johnson What?

Bunyans You know. A well-timed hook through the leg trap.

Johnson I've never told that to anyone before. And she used to imitate me behind my back, as I discovered by periodically turning on my heel as I left the room. And the way she ate her salad. She was a nibbler was Brenda.

Bunyans I was surprised by it myself.

Johnson Astonished.

Bunyans No surprised, it happened when I least expected it. She went at it like rabbits.

Johnson (*desperately*) But what are we going to do?

Bunyans I have asked myself that question my whole life and I have invariably replied, lexicography. (*He picks up a slip*) Tumescent.

Johnson Box forty-two.

Bunyans Teleautograph.

Johnson Box nine.

Bunyans, delving for slips, uncovers the same foot. Pause

Bunyans Tut. Tut.

Johnson Box forty-five.

Bunyans (*reconcealing the foot*) Tsk. Tsk.

Johnson I'm not sure that I could lend my name to what is after all hardly more than a click of the tongue.

Bunyans has heard nothing since discovering the body

Bunyans (*thoughtfully*) I see there is more in you, Johnson, than is dreamt of in our lexicography.

Johnson You know you are absolutely right. Ate salad just like a rabbit. The first time I saw her eating celery, I experienced an appalling sense of loss.

Bunyans Was it your celery?

Johnson (*glowering at him*) You misunderstand me. Is it deliberate?

Bunyans By no manner of means.

Bunyans What kind of shoes was she wearing?

Johnson Oh—this is some twelve years ago, you must remember . . .

Bunyans No. No. Today. At lunch. When you and Brenda had a rift within your lute.

Johnson (*vaguely evasive*) Oh . . . our spat.

Bunyans Not that it's of any consequence.

Johnson (*hysterically*) What's wrong with you, Bunyans? Why this talk of shoes and celery? We're wasting time, man!
Bunyans You brought up the celery.
Johnson Never mind who brought it up—we have to get on! We have to start! We have to finish! I'm going mad.
Bunyans Get a grip on yourself, Johnson! I've never known you crack like this before.
Johnson I'm dying!
Bunyans Why?
Johnson I'm old!
Bunyans You're not.
Johnson We must work.
Bunyans We have to clear all this first. (*He indicates the piles of slips still scattered around the room*)
Johnson Well then. (*Panting, he bends down and heaves an armful of slips from the floor and dumps them on the table*) There.
Bunyans It's no good just . . .

But Johnson does it again

Johnson Yes! There!

Bunyans unwillingly joins him in gathering armfuls of slips and dumping them

Bunyans Oh, Johnson, this is not the methodical man I used to know.
Johnson I've been methodical too long. We must finish.

He looks around him. They have cleared some of the floor now so that the mound that covers Brenda stands in isolation

Isn't that better?
Bunyans (*doubtfully*) Ye-es. But . . .
Johnson No. No "buts". To the typewriter.
Bunyans We won't have all the words.
Johnson Can either of us type?
Bunyans Not that I know of.

There is silence as they avoid each others' eye

She used to do that.
Johnson (*irritably*) Yes, yes, yes, yes, yes. There's no need to . . .
Bunyans I'll . . .
Johnson One can but try.

He approaches the typewriter warily. He looks down at it—he looks up at Fowler, then quickly away again

Bunyans (*in a rush*) There's those over there.
Johnson What? Oh yes. Good heavens. Oh . . .
Bunyans A couple, no more.
Johnson Too many. Get into those and . . .
Bunyans We'd never get finished.
Johnson Leave them, leave them. Have we not got enough? (*He indicates the boxes expansively*)
Bunyans Too many.
Johnson Exactly. What do they think we are. We must start. We must finish.

Bunyans sits at the typewriter. Johnson takes the first card from the first box

"T". The Twentieth letter from the English and other modern alphabets. The nineteenth of the ancient Roman alphabet, corresponding in form to the Greek "Tau", from the Phoenician and ancient Semitic.
Bunyans Wait, wait, wait.
Johnson (*looking up from the slip*) What is it?
Bunyans You're going too fast.
Johnson Where have you got to?
Bunyans "T".
Johnson Is that all? Dear Christ, is this the pace at which we shall proceed?
Bunyans I am unfamiliar with the organization of the keyboard. It's eccentrically arranged.
Johnson It has letters of the alphabet, I presume?
Bunyans But not in order. "Qwertyuiop".
Johnson Dear God in Heaven, a faulty machine!
Bunyans We need a typist. We need . . . (*He breaks off awkwardly*)

Johnson No, no, no. Certainly not. You mustn't ... To tell the truth, I like it better without her. I mean ... well ... it's quieter.
Bunyans Certainly. One could hear a pin drop.
Johnson You remember how she used to jabber? I used to wonder what she found to talk about.
Bunyans What did she talk about?

Johnson shrugs

Johnson I never listened. (*In despair*) What are we going to do?
Bunyans (*succinctly*) Get a typist. A male typist. Or at least androgynous. Tomorrow. (*Grandly*) It doesn't make any difference to me, I must say, her not being here.
Johnson Nor me. I never liked her. Not per se. I *liked* her well enough. Early on in our relationship. But latterly ... I wouldn't mind if she was ... how does one say it?
Bunyans Not here?
Johnson Departed.
Bunyans Defunct.
Johnson Demised.
Bunyans Deceased.
Johnson Stiff.
Bunyans Kicked the bucket.
Johnson Dead.

A collective sigh is heard from the small crowd out of sight. A batsman has skied a ball. Bunyans and Johnson look at the window where the man on the square leg boundary, outside the library window, starts positioning himself under the catch which he takes cleanly. There is applause from without

The two men turn away and continue

Johnson Tizzy.
Bunyans That's a start. Box twenty-three. Titoki to Toggery.

In the following passage the two men cravenly attempt to establish that each is willing to condone the other. But they get nowhere and end in a silent morass of mutual bafflement

Johnson I am not a violent man in point of fact.

Bunyans Of course you're not. I know that.

Johnson Nor are you a violent man—I know that—if you, ever did a violent thing, then there would be a good reason—I mean I would understand—see the other fellow's predicament—tolerance—

Bunyans Live and let live . . .

Bunyans
Johnson } (*simultaneously*) So to speak.

Bunyans And were *you* ever to be even momentarily violent——

Johnson Which I wouldn't—but I would be understanding were *you*, due to the impulsiveness of youth, to be momentarily violent.

Bunyans Though I am not a violent man.

Johnson As I well know.

Bunyans In other words.

Johnson Exactly my point. (*Pause*)

Bunyans (*picking up a slip glumly; without passion*) This is one of hers. Tampon—iron plate with spikes for walking on ice. (*He throws it away, more in sorrow than in anger*) I blame you for this, Johnson.

Johnson (*defensively*) I couldn't be looking over her shoulder all the time.

Bunyans has picked up another galleyproof

Bunyans Crampon . . . A thin griddle cake made of flour, beaten egg and milk . . . We're ruined. We're going to have to go back over everything.

Johnson I'm sorry, but when I proposed to Brenda all those years ago, it was with the promise—the dream—of sharing everything, working side by side . . .

Bunyans You should have had the grace to share *her* work and not let her share *ours*.

Johnson (*angrily*) How could I be a money changer in a pinball parlour?

Bunyans Pinball . . .?

Johnson I got a double first in . . . what the hell was it?

Bunyans (*shouting*) Pinball machines . . .

Johnson (*shouting*) Rubbish . . .

Bunyans No—we went from pinaster to pinze-nez.

Johnson (*stopped in his tracks*) By God you're right. Take this down. Pinball machine. American, twentieth cent.—a machine . . .

Bunyans A device . . .

Johnson A device consisting of—God help us . . .

Bunyans An automatic bagatel board in which the players by releasing . . .

Johnson Projecting . . .

Bunyans Propelling . . .

Johnson By means of a spring-controlled plunger.

Bunyans Balls. God damn it.

Johnson The fact of the matter is she used the same teabag three or four times, five in the case of my aged and inoffensive sister. Did you know that?

Bunyans No—I knew about her earwax, but not about the teabags.

Johnson She was a slut . . .

Bunyans A boring old baggage . . .

Johnson (*with contempt*) And the way she was always trying to adulterate the dictionary—

Bunyans Moronic bunny-slippered slag . . .

Johnson . . . spurious words . . . cosmodrome . . . payload . . . aero-space . . . bleep . . . blip . . . megadeath . . .

Bunyans Refusing to shave . . .

Johnson (*contemptuously*) We have go—

Bunyans And her drawers—never found anything in them.

Johnson And she was less than scrupulous about her feet to-boot.

Bunyans Her bu'nyons. If you hadn't done it, I would have done it.

Johnson And I would have if you hadn't.

Bunyans So would I.

Johnson But you did.

Bunyans No *you* did. This is no time for shilly-shallying, Johnson. The teabags alone condone your action. Condemned out of her own spout.

Johnson You are rambling, man. Raving. Corybantic. Maddened, no doubt, by guilt, you have suffered the loosening of a screw.

Bunyans Guilt?

Johnson At killing my wife. My dear fellow—think nothing of it . . .

Bunyans You killed her. I saw her foot. No doubt in jealous rage . . .

Johnson You said yourself you could kill her—because of the octaroon with ground almonds . . .

From under the papers comes a cry

Brenda Enough!

Johnson and Bunyans stare at the paper, which convulses and Brenda emerges

Enough of this virago.

Bunyans Brenda—you're alive!

Johnson (*muttering*) It *was* bunglers. (*Louder*) My sugar dumpling.

Brenda Don't try to sweet-shop me, you sea-lion old taxicographer!

Johnson Brenda—I assure you——

Brenda I returned from a state of inconsequence several minutes ago . . . eardropping on your conversation as I drifted back from the barn from which no traveller returns, back from the valley of the château of death, I heard every syllabub of your farinaceous attack on my parson.

Johnson You were dreaming.

Brenda Liar! Lying hypnotist.

Johnson Your personal hygiene is immaculate, your breasts are like twin roses.

Brenda Philatelist!!

Johnson And your scholarship—your range—how shall I put it?

Brenda Syncopated groveller.

Johnson Your grasp of—to put it in plain English—*le mot juste*.

Brenda I want go.

Johnson If you want go, you shall have go.

Bunyans I'll help you pack.

Johnson And I'll carry your boring old baggage.

Brenda I will not stand here and be pillarised and vitrified. I have demoted my life to toxicology and slavering over a hot stove and this is the thanks I get. My late lamentable mother saw you for the hypocritical greasy piccolo that you have proven yourself to be. But you incinerated yourself into my affectations with your swarthy talk and I succumbed to your brandysnaps. I could have made a tureen for myself. You thought you could pack me up and cast me aside like a wartime truss. There was more to me than that before taxidermatory and Bognor Regis wore me down to my eccles. I can insure you. Even on V.E. night you disbanded me during the hunky-dory. (*Indicating Bunyans*) Not that he's any better. He's no gentlemen. Corsetry—he doesn't know the meaning of the word—and don't think there weren't a frenzy of other suitors, but I was never a croquette. I have been fidelitous to a fault. And now I am repaid by a vivacious blow on the head by a man whom I have allowed to play ducks and drakes with my body for thirty years.

Johnson
Bunyans } (*together*) I deny it.

Brenda (*rubbing her head*) I still have the confusion to show for it.

Johnson We entered and found you lying under the papers. The whole place was in chaos.

Brenda It was perfectly tidy when I entered this room in search of the crampon which I recalled leaving half-finished with my elevenses. (*She has a half-eaten crumpet*) Ah I remember now, I saw it on the bookshelf. (*She moves towards the bookshelf*) I took one pace towards it and suddenly ...

There is a crash of breaking glass

All three heads jerk towards the french window; there is now a second broken pane and Brenda is lying on the floor as the ball rolls to a stop. The two men look at her and then at the window

The cricketer from before is opening the window

Immediately there is a noise of wind, and papers begin blowing everywhere as in a snowstorm

The cricketer has, meanwhile, walked into the room and picked up the ball with a furtive look at the chaos he has (for the second time) unwittingly caused

He leaves the room by the window, which he closes behind him

Bunyans and Johnson go over to Brenda. Johnson finds her hand to take her pulse

Bunyans We have go?
Johnson She has went.

Black-out

FURNITURE AND PROPERTY LIST

On stage: French windows with a broken pane of glass
Desk
Table
Chair
Television set, showing a cricket match being played
Telescope on a tripod
Old-fashioned telephone
Typewriter
Bookshelves containing boxes and a copy of *Fowler's Modern English Usage*
Dictionary
Piles of paper and galleyproofs

Off stage: Cricket ball (**Stage Management**)

Personal: **Brenda**: half-eaten crumpet

LIGHTING PLOT

Property fittings required: nil
Interior. The same throughout

To open: General interior lighting

Cue 1 **Johnson:** "She has went" (Page 19)
Fade to black-out

EFFECTS PLOT

Cue 1 To open (Page 1)
The sound of a TV cricket post-mortem

Cue 2 **Johnson** dials 3 digits (Page 2)
Crackling telephone conversation with operator as per page 2

Cue 3 **Johnson:** "Dead" (Page 14)
A collective sigh from crowd off followed by applause

Cue 4 **Brenda:** " . . . one pace towards it and suddenly . . ." (Page 18)
Sound of breaking glass

Cue 5 The cricketer opens the window (Page 18)
Noise and effect of wind

Cue 6 The cricketer leaves the room (Page 18)
Wind effect ends